The Ultimate British Prime Ministers Quiz

B.R. Egginton

Contents

Preface..3

Questions...5

Answers...66

Preface

The United Kingdom has long boasted its status as the home of the world's longest continually functioning parliament. Yet the office of Prime Minister is a considerably more recent invention.

Spawned out of the gradual decline of the English monarchy – from the signing of the Magna Carta in 1215 to the English Civil War and the Glorious Revolution over four hundred years later – the term was first attributed to Robert Walpole in the eighteenth century.

Since then the role of the Prime Minister has evolved rapidly: growing in its power, publicity and democratic accountability.

What all its holders have in common is bearing the burden of guiding one of the most powerful nations the world has ever known through stormy seas, and yet only a fraction of these political titans are remembered by the general public today.

Like most towering figures of any day or age, the world has moved swiftly on from their passing, and over time their names and deeds have been forgotten: often at great loss, for it is through their triumphs and failures that we can progress… and prevent decline.

Therefore, when you open this book do not merely think of it as means of testing your knowledge of a tireless succession of grey-haired well-to-do aristocrats. Instead, open your eyes, think outside the box and envisage it as the key to unlocking the remarkable story of the United Kingdom: its formation, its unprecedented rise to the top of the world's food chain and its equally unprecedented demise.

Unlike the British Empire, make sure the sun never sets on your intellectual endeavours.

Questions

Robert Walpole (easy)

1. Robert Walpole was the Earl of what?

A Warwick
B Oxford
C Surrey
D Essex

2. What nickname was given to Robert Walpole's period of political dominance?

A The Premiership
B The Regency
C The Robinocracy
D The Interregnum

3. How many times did Robert Walpole marry?

A 0
B 1
C 2
D 3

4. What political faction was Robert Walpole a member of?

A Whig
B Tory
C Peelite
D Liberal

5. Robert Walpole was born in which English county?

A Middlesex
B Staffordshire
C Somerset
D Norfolk

6. How many siblings did Robert Walpole have?

A 0
B 3
C 6
D 18

7. Where was Robert Walpole imprisoned in 1712?

A Newgate Prison
B Kensington Palace
C Tower of London
D Hampton Court

8. In what year was Robert Walpole appointed First Lord of the Treasury, Chancellor of the Exchequer and Leader of the House of Commons?

A 1699
B 1712
C 1721
D 1734

9. Which social group was Robert Walpole's main support base?

A Peasantry
B Merchants
C Clergy
D Country gentry

10. The War of Jenkins' Ear was fought between the United Kingdom and which other country?

A Prussia
B France
C Spain
D Portugal

Robert Walpole (average)

1. Robert Walpole served as Prime Minister under which two monarchs?
2. As a young man, Robert Walpole purchased shares in what joint-stock company?
3. Robert Walpole used his influence to prevent Britain entering what war in 1733?
4. Robert Walpole was a close friend of which Queen?
5. What party was formed in 1725 to oppose Robert Walpole's government?
6. In what year did Robert Walpole resign as Prime Minister?
7. How was Catherine Shorter related to Robert Walpole?
8. What career did Robert Walpole originally plan on pursuing?
9. What residence was Robert Walpole offered by the king as a gift in 1732?
10. The Walpole collection is a collection of what?

Robert Walpole (expert)

1. Which constituent college of Cambridge University did Robert Walpole study at?
2. Which house did Robert Walpole commission the construction of in 1722?
3. Robert Walpole won a seat for which parliamentary constituency in 1701?
4. Upon becoming Prime Minister, Robert Walpole had to deal with a financial crisis caused by what?
5. In what year did Robert Walpole die?
6. Why was Robert Walpole briefly imprisoned in 1712?
7. Robert Walpole was nicknamed Sir what?
8. In what year did Robert Walpole become an Earl?
9. Which nursery rhyme is sometimes connected to the fall of Robert Walpole's government?
10. Walpole Island, named after Robert Walpole, is located in which Canadian province?

Spencer Compton (average)

1. In what years did Spencer Compton serve as Prime Minister?
2. Which university did Spencer Compton study at?
3. Spencer Compton is buried in which country manor?
4. Spencer Compton's father, James Compton, was an ardent supporter of which side during the English Civil War?
5. How many times did Spencer Compton marry?
6. Spencer Compton was born in which English county?
7. In what year did Spencer Compton first become a Member of Parliament?
8. What political position was Spencer Compton appointed to in 1715?
9. Spencer Compton hired which Scottish architect to rebuild Compton Place?
10. Spencer Compton was Earl of what?

Henry Pelham (average)

1. How was Henry Pelham related to Thomas Pelham-Holles?
2. Which English county was Henry Pelham born in?
3. What was the name of Henry Pelham's wife?
4. Which constituent college of Oxford University was Henry Pelham educated at?
5. Which group led a major uprising in 1745?
6. Henry Pelham became a founding governor of which children's home in 1739?
7. What house did Henry Pelham have built after he became Prime Minister?
8. Henry Pelham was the first Prime Minister not to accede to what social group during his lifetime?
9. How many children did Henry Pelham have?
10. What political party was Henry Pelham a member of?

Thomas Pelham-Holles (average)

1. Thomas Pelham-Holles was born in what city?
2. Thomas Pelham-Holles was Duke of what?
3. Which boarding school did Thomas Pelham-Holles study at?
4. What was the name of Thomas Pelham-Holles's wife?
5. What political office was Thomas Pelham-Holles appointed to in 1717?
6. How many times did Thomas Pelham-Holles serve as Prime Minister?
7. What island did the United Kingdom lose to France in 1756?
8. Who was King when Thomas Pelham-Holles fell from power in 1762?
9. What political position did Thomas Pelham-Holles hold during Charles Watson-Wentworth's premiership?
10. Which major war did the United Kingdom fight against France during Thomas Pelham-Holles's premiership?

John Stuart (average)

1. John Stuart was born in what city?
2. What political party was John Stuart a member of?
3. What university did John Stuart study at?
4. John Stuart was Earl of what?
5. John Stuart was named the first President of what in 1780?
6. Who did John Stuart elope with in 1735?
7. In what year was the Treaty of Paris signed, ending the Seven Years' War?
8. Which flowering plant genus is named after John Stuart?
9. What was the name of the mansion John Stuart purchased in 1763?
10. John Stuart died near which London square?

George Grenville (average)

1. George Grenville was first elected as a Member of Parliament for which Parliamentary constituency?
2. In what year was the Stamp Act passed?
3. Which King dismissed George Grenville as Prime Minister?
4. How was George Grenville related to William Grenville?
5. What house was George Grenville born at?
6. Who did George Grenville's sister, Hester, marry?
7. In his early political career, George Grenville was one of Cobham's Cubs. Who was their patron?
8. What was George Grenville's occupation prior to becoming a politician?
9. George Grenville had which radical journalist prosecuted shortly after becoming Prime Minister?
10. What cabinet position was George Grenville appointed to in 1762?

Charles Watson-Wentworth (average)

1. Charles Watson-Wentworth was Marquess of what?
2. How many times did Charles Watson-Wentworth serve as Prime Minister?
3. Where is Charles Watson-Wentworth buried?
4. What was the name of the country house where Charles Watson-Wentworth was raised?
5. The Declaratory Act accompanied the repeal of which 1765 act?
6. Charles Watson-Wentworth died during an epidemic of what disease?
7. Who inherited Charles Watson-Wentworth's estates after his death?
8. Who proposed the Relief of the Poor Act 1782?
9. Which Irish statesman and author of *A Vindication of Natural Society* was a close friend of Charles Watson-Wentworth?
10. Charles Watson-Wentworth's father made him a colonel during what uprising?

William Pitt the Elder (average)

1. William Pitt the Elder was known as 'The Great...' what?
2. William Pitt the Elder served as Prime Minister in what years?
3. What political party was William Pitt the Elder a member of?
4. Where is William Pitt the Elder buried?
5. William Pitt the Elder's grandfather, Thomas Pitt, was well-known for acquiring what precious object?
6. William Pitt the Elder was Earl of what?
7. What did William Pitt the Elder embark on shortly after leaving Oxford University without a degree?
8. Before becoming a politician, William Pitt the Elder worked in what field?
9. In what year did William Pitt the Elder deliver his maiden speech in the House of Commons?
10. The Pitt–Newcastle ministry governed the United Kingdom at the height of what war?

Augustus FitzRoy (average)

1. How old was Augustus FitzRoy when he became Prime Minister?
2. What was the name of the house that Augustus FitzRoy died in?
3. What was the occupation of Augustus FitzRoy's father?
4. Augustus FitzRoy was Duke of what?
5. Who did Augustus FitzRoy divorce in 1769?
6. Augustus FitzRoy was widely criticised for allowing France to annex what island?
7. Augustus FitzRoy served as Chancellor of what university?
8. Who did Augustus FitzRoy famously have an affair with in 1764?
9. Augustus FitzRoy was a descendant of which English King?
10. In what year did Augustus FitzRoy step down as Prime Minister?

Frederick North (average)

1. Frederick North led the United Kingdom through the majority of what war?
2. How was William Legge related to Frederick North?
3. In what year was Frederick North first elected as a Member of Parliament?
4. What was the name of Frederick North's wife?
5. What islands did Spain attempt to seize from the United Kingdom in 1770?
6. The Armada of 1779 was a naval enterprise carried out by what two countries?
7. What was the name of the coalition that was formed in 1783?
8. As Prime Minister, Frederick North was associated with what political party?
9. The Gordon Riots of 1780 were targeted against what religious group?
10. Frederick North had completely lost what by the time he entered the House of Lords in 1790?

William Petty (average)

1. William Petty was born in what city?
2. In what years did William Petty serve as Prime Minister?
3. William Petty was the Earl of what?
4. What political position did William Petty hold during William Pitt the Elder's premiership?
5. How many times did William Petty marry?
6. What constituent college of Oxford University was William Petty educated at?
7. Richard Oswald negotiated which peace agreement?
8. William Petty took part in an amphibious attempt to capture which French port in 1757?
9. What military rank did William Petty reach in 1783?
10. After leaving university, William Petty served in an army regiment commanded by what famous military officer?

William Cavendish-Bentinck (average)

1. William Cavendish-Bentinck served as Chancellor of what university?
2. How long was the gap between William Cavendish-Bentinck's two terms as Prime Minister?
3. How is William Cavendish-Bentinck related to Elizabeth II?
4. What church is William Cavendish-Bentinck buried in?
5. William Cavendish-Bentinck was Duke of what?
6. What Parliamentary constituency was William Cavendish-Bentinck elected to represent in 1761?
7. What two politicians dominated William Cavendish-Bentinck's first term as Prime Minister?
8. What major treaty was signed in 1783?
9. William Cavendish-Bentinck died after an operation to remove what?
10. What conflict broke out between France and Spain during William Cavendish-Bentinck's second term as Prime Minister?

William Pitt the Younger (easy)

1. How old was William Pitt the Younger when he became Prime Minister?

A 24
B 29
C 38
D 46

2. How many times did William Pitt the Younger marry?

A 0
B 1
C 2
D 3

3. How many times did William Pitt the Younger serve as Prime Minister?

A 1
B 2
C 3
D 4

4. Who was King during William Pitt the Younger's tenure as Prime Minister?

A George II
B George III
C William III
D Edward VI

5. Even though he is commonly referred to as a Tory, how did William Pitt the Younger describe his political affiliation?

A Roundhead
B Liberal
C Monarchist
D Independent Whig

6. What conflict broke out during William Pitt the Younger's premiership?

A Boer Wars
B Crimean War
C Napoleonic Wars
D American Revolutionary War

7. The Acts of Union 1800 united what two kingdoms?

A England and Scotland
B Great Britain and Ireland
C Great Britain and Canada
D Scotland and Ireland

8. Where is William Pitt the Younger buried?

A Westminster Abbey
B St Paul's Cathedral
C York Minster
D Buckingham Palace

9. What university was William Pitt the Younger educated at?

A Harvard University
B University of St Andrews
C Oxford University
D Cambridge University

10. William Pitt the Younger's mother, Hester, was the sister of which former Prime Minister?

A Robert Walpole
B George Grenville
C John Stuart
D Charles Watson-Wentworth

William Pitt the Younger (average)

1. William Pitt the Younger attended university from what age?
2. William Pitt the Younger was a close friend of what famous abolitionist?
3. When he first became a Member of Parliament, William Pitt the Younger was a vocal critic of what war?
4. William Pitt the Younger first served as Chancellor of the Exchequer under what Prime Minister?
5. What offer from the King did William Pitt the Younger decline in 1783?
6. Which Whig politician was William Pitt the Younger's arch rival?
7. The India Act 1784 reorganised what major company?
8. What constituent country of the United Kingdom rebelled in 1798?
9. What major naval battle did the United Kingdom fight against France and Spain in 1805?
10. How many children did William Pitt the Younger have?

William Pitt the Younger (expert)

1. What was the first Parliamentary constituency that William Pitt the Younger represented as a Member of Parliament?
2. What was the name of the coalition that governed the United Kingdom immediately before William Pitt the Younger's rise to power?
3. The Triple Alliance of 1788 was a military alliance between the United Kingdom and what two other countries?
4. In what year did William Pitt the Younger resign as Prime Minister?
5. Which politician published a biography about William Pitt the Younger in 2004?
6. What title did William Pitt the Younger's father hold?
7. What occupation did William Pitt the Younger pursue before becoming a politician?
8. What was the name of William Pitt the Younger's older brother?
9. William Pitt the Younger introduced what kind of tax for the first time?
10. William Pitt the Younger resigned as Prime Minister over what issue?

Henry Addington (average)

1. The Treaty of Amiens of 1802 temporarily ended hostilities between the United Kingdom and what other country?
2. What cabinet position did Henry Addington occupy between 1812 and 1822?
3. In what years did Henry Addington serve as Prime Minister?
4. In what year did Henry Addington become Speaker of the House of Commons?
5. What was the occupation of Henry Addington's father, Anthony Addington?
6. Henry Addington was first elected to Parliament as a representative of what constituency?
7. What peerage did Henry Addington receive?
8. What massacre took place in Manchester in 1819?
9. What is the name of the house where Henry Addington died?
10. Henry Addington donated four acres of land to what town?

William Grenville (average)

1. How many years did William Grenville serve as Prime Minister?
2. What political office did William Grenville's father hold?
3. What cabinet position did William Grenville hold between 1789 and 1791?
4. What rank of nobility did William Grenville possess?
5. What was the name of the government of national unity that William Grenville formed after becoming Prime Minister?
6. What did William Grenville's government ban in 1807?
7. William Grenville served as Chancellor of what university?
8. What English county was William Grenville born in?
9. What was the name of William Grenville's wife?
10. At the time of his death William Grenville's arboretum contained the largest collection of what type of tree in Britain?

Spencer Perceval (average)

1. What happened to Spencer Perceval in 1812?
2. How was Jane Wilson related to Spencer Perceval?
3. What was Spencer Perceval's occupation prior to becoming a politician?
4. In 1796 Spencer Perceval became the Member of Parliament for what Parliamentary constituency?
5. In what year did Spencer Perceval become Chancellor of the Exchequer?
6. In what year was John Bellingham executed?
7. Who served as Home Secretary under Spencer Perceval?
8. The Walcheren Campaign was an unsuccessful British expedition to what country?
9. Which radical Member of Parliament was imprisoned in the Tower of London during Spencer Perceval's premiership?
10. How many children did Spencer Perceval have?

Robert Jenkinson (average)

1. Robert Jenkinson was the Earl of what?
2. In what year did the Peterloo Massacre occur?
3. What political party was Robert Jenkinson a member of?
4. What monarchs did Robert Jenkinson serve as Prime Minister under?
5. What was the name of the war the United Kingdom fought against the United States of America during Robert Jenkinson's premiership?
6. What diplomatic meeting took place between 1814 and 1815 with the intention of creating a long-term peace plan for Europe?
7. What controversial laws were enforced in the United Kingdom between 1815 and 1846?
8. What school did Robert Jenkinson attend as a child?
9. Robert Jenkinson first served as a cabinet minister under which Prime Minister?
10. In what year did Robert Jenkinson first secure a seat in the House of Commons?

George Canning (average)

1. George Canning served as the United Kingdom's ambassador to what country between 1814 and 1816?
2. In what year did George Canning serve as Prime Minister?
3. Where is George Canning buried?
4. What political party was George Canning a member of?
5. What was the name of George Canning's wife?
6. George Canning won a prize in 1789 for writing what poem?
7. What was the occupation of George Canning's mother, Mary Ann Costello?
8. George Canning helped to establish what newspaper in 1797?
9. George Canning became Treasurer of what in 1804?
10. Who did George Canning fight a duel with in 1809?

Frederick John Robinson (average)

1. In what year did Frederick John Robinson become Chancellor of the Exchequer?
2. What county was Frederick John Robinson born in?
3. Who did Fredrick John Robinson marry in 1814?
4. After graduating in 1802, Frederick John Robinson was admitted to which of London's four Inns of the Court?
5. What position did Henry Petty-Fitzmaurice hold in Frederick John Robinson's cabinet?
6. What peerage did Frederick John Robinson receive in 1833?
7. When Frederick John Robinson served as President of the Board of Trade between 1841 and 1843, which future Prime Minister was his deputy?
8. Frederick John Robinson first served as a Member of Parliament for which Parliamentary constituency?
9. In what years did Fredrick John Robinson serve as Prime Minister?
10. Frederick John Robinson's residence on Old Burlington Street was attacked when what controversial laws were going through Parliament?

Arthur Wellesley (easy)

1. Arthur Wellesley was Duke of what?

A Wellington
B Edinburgh
C Norfolk
D Northumberland

2. How many times did Arthur Wellesley serve as Prime Minister?

A 1
B 2
C 3
D 4

3. Arthur Wellesley was born in what city?

A London
B Edinburgh
C Paris
D Dublin

4. What political party was Arthur Wellesley a member of?

A Independent
B Whig
C Tory
D Liberal

5. Arthur Wellesley famously led coalition forces at which 1815 battle?

A Battle of Trafalgar
B Battle of Waterloo
C Battle of Edgecote Moor
D Battle of the Saintes

6. What rank did Arthur Wellesley reach in the British Army?

A Colonel
B General
C Corporal
D Field Marshal

7. Arthur Wellesley served as the British ambassador to what country between 1814 and 1815?

A Austria
B USA
C Prussia
D France

8. Where is Arthur Wellesley buried?

A Canterbury Cathedral
B York Minster
C Westminster Abbey
D St Paul's Cathedral

9. In what year did Arthur Wellesley join the British Army?

A 1776
B 1787
C 1794
D 1801

10. Which famous Royal Navy officer did Arthur Wellesley meet shortly after returning from military service in India?

A John Jervis
B Horatio Nelson
C Cuthbert Collingwood
D James Cook

Arthur Wellesley (average)

1. Arthur Wellesley served as Prime Minister under which two monarchs?
2. Arthur Wellesley rose to prominence as a general during which campaign of the Napoleonic Wars?
3. What was the name of Arthur Wellesley's wife?
4. What boarding school did Arthur Wellesley study at between 1781 and 1784?
5. The Siege of Seringapatam 1799 was a confrontation between the East India Company and the Kingdom of Mysore in what war?
6. The Battle of Assaye was fought between the East India Company and what empire?
7. In what country did the Battle of Talavera take place?
8. Who composed the orchestral work *Wellington's Victory*?
9. Arthur Wellesley played a key role in establishing what university in 1829?
10. Arthur Wellesley was nicknamed Iron what?

Arthur Wellesley (expert)

1. Arthur Wellesley died in what fort?
2. What was the name of Arthur Wellesley's ancestral home?
3. Arthur Wellesley's elder brother, Richard Wellesley, held what political position between 1821 and 1828?
4. What order of chivalry did Arthur Wellesley receive for his service in India?
5. In what year was Arthur Wellesley elected a Member of Parliament for Rye?
6. Who did Arthur Wellesley fight in a duel in 1829?
7. Arthur Wellesley was a close friend of what diarist?
8. Arthur Wellesley disliked travelling by train after witnessing which politician get run over by Robert Stephenson's *Rocket*?
9. Alfred Stevens is best known as the sculptor of what?
10. Arthur Wellesley was appointed to what position in 1827?

Charles Grey (average)

1. Charles Grey was a member of what political party?
2. Charles Grey was born in which English county?
3. In what year did Charles Grey become Prime Minister?
4. The Great Reform Act is known by what other name?
5. Charles Grey attended which constituent college of Cambridge University?
6. In what year was slavery banned throughout the British Empire?
7. How many children did Charles Grey have with his wife?
8. What was the name of the illegitimate daughter Charles Grey had with Georgiana Cavendish, Duchess of Devonshire?
9. What drink is named after Charles Grey?
10. Grey's Monument is located in the centre of which English city?

William Lamb (average)

1. William Lamb served as Prime Minister under which two monarchs?
2. What political party was William Lamb a member of?
3. What position did William Lamb hold in Charles Grey's cabinet?
4. William Lamb was the last Prime Minister to be dismissed by who?
5. What occupation did William Lamb go into after leaving university?
6. What was the first constituency William Lamb represented as a Member of Parliament?
7. William Lamb's wife, Lady Caroline Lamb, was well-known for having an affair with who?
8. What noble title did William Lamb hold?
9. What house did William Lamb die at?
10. The Bedchamber crisis occurred in 1839 after William Lamb announced his intention to do what?

Robert Peel (average)

1. What did Robert Peel play a key role in creating in 1829?
2. How many times did Robert Peel serve as Home Secretary?
3. Robert Peel served as a Member of Parliament for what university constituency?
4. What two nicknames were police officers given in honour of Robert Peel?
5. In what year did Robert Peel first become Prime Minister?
6. What political manifesto did Robert Peel issue shortly after becoming Prime Minister?
7. The Mines and Collieries Act 1842 prohibited children under what age from working underground in coal mines?
8. What Act of Parliament relating to railways was passed in 1844?
9. Who attempted to assassinate Robert Peel in 1843?
10. Robert Peel resigned as Prime Minister after repealing what controversial tariffs?

John Russell (average)

1. John Russell served as Prime Minister for which two political parties?
2. What country suffered from a major famine during John Russell's first term as Prime Minister?
3. What political position did John Russell hold during the American Civil War?
4. What mansion did John Russell die in?
5. What university did John Russell attend?
6. While travelling in Europe in December 1814, John Russell met which famous military leader and statesman?
7. What nickname did John Russell acquire during his fight for the Representation of the People Act 1832?
8. The Don Pacifico affair was an episode of what type of diplomacy?
9. What position did Henry John Temple hold during John Russell's first term as Prime Minister?
10. John Russell became Prime Minister for the second time following the death of what statesman?

Edward Smith-Stanley (average)

1. Edward Smith-Stanley was the Earl of what?
2. How many times did Edward Smith-Stanley serve as Prime Minister?
3. What political party was Edward Smith-Stanley a member of?
4. What 1867 act enfranchised part of the urban male working class for the first time?
5. What was Edward Smith-Stanley's ancestral home?
6. Who served as Chancellor of the Exchequer under Edward Smith-Stanley?
7. What name was given to the ministry Edward Smith-Stanley formed in 1852?
8. The Sepoy Mutiny of 1857 ended whose rule in India?
9. Edward Smith-Stanley served as the leader of what for almost 22 years?
10. The Stanley Letter outlined Edward Smith-Stanley's vision to establish legal basis for what in Ireland?

George Hamilton-Gordon (average)

1. The United Kingdom entered what war during George Hamilton-Gordon's premiership?
2. In what years did George Hamilton-Gordon serve as Prime Minister?
3. George Hamilton-Gordon was the Earl of what?
4. What happened to George Hamilton-Gordon at the age of 11?
5. What cabinet level position was George Hamilton-Gordon appointed to in 1828?
6. What did George Hamilton-Gordon's first wife, Lady Catherine Hamilton, die from in 1812?
7. George Hamilton-Gordon was appointed as the United Kingdom's ambassador to what country in 1813?
8. George Hamilton-Gordon served as the Chancellor of what in 1828?
9. George Hamilton-Gordon was a member of what faction of the Conservative Party?
10. What famous charge took place during the Battle of Balaclava in 1854?

Henry John Temple (easy)

1. What title did Henry John Temple hold?

A Baron Stuart
B Duke of Marlborough
C Earl of Warwick
D Viscount Palmerston

2. Henry John Temple was the first person from which political party to serve as Prime Minister?

A Conservative
B Liberal
C Labour
D Whig

3. How many times did Henry John Temple serve as Prime Minister?

A 1
B 2
C 3
D 4

4. Where is Henry John Temple buried?

A Westminster Abbey
B St Paul's Cathedral
C Canterbury Cathedral
D York Minster

5. Henry John Temple's wife, Emily, was the sister of which Prime Minister?

A William Gladstone
B Robert Peel
C Arthur Wellesley
D William Lamb

6. Henry John Temple served as Prime Minister under which monarch?

A William IV
B George V
C Victoria
D Edward VII

7. Henry John Temple became Prime Minister during what war?

A American Revolutionary War
B War of the Austrian Succession
C Crimean War
D Peninsular War

8. Where was Henry John Temple born?

A Westminster
B Warwick
C Winchester
D Wolverhampton

9. What cabinet level position did Henry John Temple hold three times?

A Secretary of State for War
B Foreign Secretary
C Home Secretary
D Chancellor of the Exchequer

10. How many legitimate children did Henry John Temple father?

A 0
B 1
C 5
D 12

Henry John Temple (average)

1. What was the name of the country house Henry John Temple had built near the Irish village of Cliffoney?
2. Henry John Temple was defeated in an election for what Parliamentary constituency in 1806?
3. Who was Prime Minister when Henry John Temple was Leader of the Opposition?
4. Henry John Temple supported what kind of diplomacy?
5. How old was Henry John Temple when he became Prime Minister?
6. What war broke out between the United Kingdom and the Qing dynasty in 1856?
7. The Matrimonial Causes Act 1857 made it easier to do what?
8. The Orsini affair refers to an attempt to assassinate who with a British made bomb?
9. What position did William Gladstone hold on Henry John Temple's cabinet?
10. The *Trent Affair* was a diplomatic incident relating to what war?

Henry John Temple (expert)

1. Why did Henry John Temple's peerage not prevent him from sitting in the House of Commons?
2. What boarding school did Henry John Temple attend?
3. In what year did Henry John Temple's father die?
4. Henry John Temple was nicknamed Lord what?
5. What is the name of the London townhouse where Henry John Temple lived?
6. Who served as the United Kingdom's ambassador to the USA during the American Civil War?
7. The CSS *Alabama* was built in what port town?
8. In what year did Henry John Temple have his last electoral victory?
9. How many people not of royal birth received a state funeral before Henry John Temple?
10. The Offences Against the Person Act was passed in what year?

Benjamin Disraeli (easy)

1. Benjamin Disraeli was the first person from what religious background to serve as Prime Minister?

A Anglican
B Catholic
C Jewish
D Mormon

2. What political party was Benjamin Disraeli a member of?

A Whig
B Liberal
C Conservative
D Labour

3. How many times did Benjamin Disraeli serve as Prime Minister?

A 1
B 2
C 3
D 4

4. Who was Benjamin Disraeli's main political rival?

A John Russell
B Henry John Temple
C William Gladstone
D William Pitt the Younger

5. In what year did Benjamin Disraeli enter the House of Commons?

A 1810
B 1837
C 1854
D 1860

6. Benjamin Disraeli maintained a close friendship with which monarch?

A William IV
B George V
C Edward VII
D Victoria

7. The Eastern Question referred to the decline of which empire?

A Russian Empire
B Ottoman Empire
C Spanish Empire
D British Empire

8. What type of conservatism did Benjamin Disraeli believe in?

A One nation conservatism
B Authoritarian conservatism
C New right conservatism
D Libertarian conservatism

9. The Cyprus Convention was an agreement with what country to cede Cyprus to the United Kingdom?

A Austria
B Egypt
C Russia
D Ottoman Empire

10. Benjamin Disraeli was born in which London district?

A City of London
B Kensington
C Fulham
D Bloomsbury

Benjamin Disraeli (average)

1. What was the name of Benjamin Disraeli's wife?
2. Benjamin Disraeli had the United Kingdom purchase a major interest in which canal company?
3. The Congress of Berlin 1878 aimed to determine territories on which peninsula?
4. In what year did Benjamin Disraeli take part in his last general election?
5. What was the original spelling of Benjamin Disraeli's surname before he had it changed?
6. How many times did Benjamin Disraeli serve as Chancellor of the Exchequer?
7. What international conference was held during the Herzegovina uprising (1875–1877)?
8. What title did Queen Victoria use from 1876 onwards?
9. Benjamin Disraeli was the Earl of what?
10. Benjamin Disraeli's family originated from what country?

Benjamin Disraeli (expert)

1. What was the name of the last novel Benjamin Disraeli published before he died?
2. In what year was Benjamin Disraeli baptised into the Church of England?
3. What club did Benjamin Disraeli join in 1836?
4. In what year did Benjamin Disraeli get married?
5. What church is Benjamin Disraeli buried in?
6. What was the name of Benjamin Disraeli's father?
7. Who published Benjamin Disraeli's first novel, *Vivian Grey*, in 1826?
8. What was the name of the country mansion that Benjamin Disraeli owned near High Wycombe, Buckinghamshire?
9. In what year did Oxford University give Benjamin Disraeli an honorary degree?
10. Who was installed as Archbishop of Canterbury in 1868?

William Gladstone (easy)

1. What was William Gladstone's middle name?

A Earl
B Edward
C Ewart
D Evan

2. William Gladstone served as Prime Minister for what political party?

A Whig
B Liberal
C Labour
D Conservative

3. How many times did William Gladstone serve as Prime Minister?

A 1
B 2
C 3
D 4

4. William Gladstone was born in what English city?

A Bristol
B Leeds
C Liverpool
D Winchester

5. Where is William Gladstone buried?

A Worcester Cathedral
B Winchester Cathedral
C York Minster
D Westminster Abbey

6. William Gladstone's parents were from what country?

A Scotland
B Wales
C England
D USA

7. What political doctrine is named after William Gladstone?

A Gladstonian democracy
B Gladstonian conservatism
C Gladstonian radicalism
D Gladstonian liberalism

8. What nickname did Benjamin Disraeli use to refer to William Gladstone?

A God's Only Mistake
B Old Bill
C Lyin' Will
D Right Honourable Fool

9. What did William Gladstone do after graduating from university?

A Emigrate to the USA
B Started his own business
C Joined the military
D Went on the Grand Tour

10. What was William Gladstone's father well-known for owning?

A A private colony
B Egyptian artefacts
C Slaves
D A ship

William Gladstone (average)

1. What was the name of William Gladstone's wife?
2. What university did William Gladstone attend?
3. While at university, what political party did William Gladstone support?
4. William Gladstone lost the index finger on his left hand while doing what?
5. William Gladstone first became Chancellor of the Exchequer under what Prime Minister?
6. William Gladstone had a rivalry with which other Prime Minister?
7. What name was given to the series of foreign policy speeches made by William Gladstone between 1878 and 1880?
8. William Gladstone resigned from Robert Peel's government in 1845 due to what grant to a Catholic seminary?
9. What church was William Gladstone a member of?
10. What side did William Gladstone support in the American Civil War?

William Gladstone (expert)

1. What two subjects did William Gladstone have a degree in?
2. In what year did William Gladstone first enter the House of Commons as a Member of Parliament?
3. William Gladstone helped to establish what college in 1847?
4. The Cardwell Reforms were a series of reforms to what?
5. What hobby did William Gladstone take up in 1858?
6. William Gladstone's coffin was transported on what transport network before his state funeral?
7. In what village is Gladstone's Library located?
8. William Gladstone was elected a Fellow of what in 1881?
9. In what year did William Gladstone first become Prime Minister?
10. What war took place between 1880 and 1881?

Robert Gascoyne-Cecil (average)

1. Robert Gascoyne-Cecil was the Marquess of what?
2. How many times did Robert Gascoyne-Cecil serve as Prime Minister?
3. What political party was Robert Gascoyne-Cecil a member of?
4. What house was Robert Gascoyne-Cecil born at?
5. Robert Gascoyne-Cecil was named Secretary of State for what in 1866?
6. In what year did Robert Gascoyne-Cecil set up London County Council?
7. What act formally adopted the two-power standard relating to naval power?
8. In 1890 the United Kingdom delivered an ultimatum to what country?
9. The Scramble for what took place during Robert Gascoyne-Cecil's premiership?
10. The Kruger telegram was a message sent from Kaiser Wilhelm II to the president of what country?

Archibald Primrose (average)

1. In what years did Archibald Primrose serve as Prime Minister?
2. Archibald Primrose was the Earl of what?
3. What country did Archibald Primrose tour in 1873, 1874 and 1876?
4. Archibald Primrose was a supporter of what faction of the Liberal Party?
5. Who was Archibald Primrose's wife?
6. Archibald Primrose was accused of having a homosexual relationship with who?
7. The vote of no confidence in Archibald Primrose's administration was known by what other name?
8. Who served as Chancellor of the Exchequer during Archibald Primrose's premiership?
9. What was the name of the horse, owned by Archibald Primrose, that won the 1894 Epsom Derby?
10. What estate did Archibald Primrose acquire as a result of his marriage?

Arthur Balfour (average)

1. Arthur Balfour served as Foreign Secretary under what Prime Minister?
2. The Balfour Declaration announced the United Kingdom's support for the establishment of a national home for what group of people?
3. What political party was Arthur Balfour a member of?
4. Arthur Balfour succeeded what relation as Prime Minister?
5. The Entente Cordiale was an agreement between the United Kingdom and what other country?
6. What war ended shortly before Arthur Balfour became Prime Minister?
7. How many times did Arthur Balfour marry?
8. In what year did Arthur Balfour first become a Member of Parliament?
9. The quartet of Arthur Balfour, Lord Randolph Churchill, Sir Henry Drummond Wolff and John Gorst were known by what name?
10. In which general election did Arthur Balfour lose his seat?

Henry Campbell-Bannerman (average)

1. Why did Henry Campbell-Bannerman resign as Prime Minister?
2. Who served as Chancellor of the Exchequer under Henry Campbell-Bannerman?
3. What country was Henry Campbell-Bannerman born in?
4. Where did Henry Campbell-Bannerman die?
5. On the day of Henry Campbell-Bannerman's death, the flag of which club was flown at half-mast?
6. What act introduced free school meals?
7. The Relugas Compact was a plot by a group of Liberal Party politicians to do what?
8. What was the name of Henry Campbell-Bannerman's wife?
9. What degree classification did Henry Campbell-Bannerman achieve at Cambridge University?
10. Henry Campbell-Bannerman served as Prime Minister under what monarch?

Herbert Henry Asquith (easy)

1. Herbert Henry Asquith was a member of what political party?

A Liberal
B Socialist
C Conservative
D Labour

2. Herbert Henry Asquith was Prime Minister for the first half of what war?

A Crimean War
B Second Boer War
C First World War
D Korean War

3. Before becoming a politician, what was Herbert Henry Asquith's occupation?

A Banker
B Merchant
C Lawyer
D Actor

4. In what year did Herbert Henry Asquith become Chancellor of the Exchequer?

A 1887
B 1905
C 1910
D 1922

5. The South Africa Act 1909 created the Union of South Africa from how many British colonies?

A 2
B 3
C 4
D 5

6. The People's Budget was a proposal to introduce unprecedented taxes on the lands and incomes of the wealthy in order to fund what?

A An updated navy
B Social welfare
C A military campaign
D The construction of a new royal residence

7. The Parliament Act 1911 partly governs the relationship between what?

A The House of Commons and the House of Lords
B The government and the opposition
C Parliament and the monarch
D Parliament and the colonies

8. How many times did Herbert Henry Asquith marry?

A 0
B 1
C 2
D 3

9. The Larne gun-running was a major gun smuggling operation organised in what country?

A England
B Scotland
C Wales
D Ireland

10. In what year did Hebert Henry Asquith form a coalition government?

A 1899
B 1902
C 1915
D 1927

Herbert Henry Asquith (average)

1. Herbert Henry Asquith served as Prime Minister under what two monarchs?
2. What English county was Herbert Henry Asquith born in?
3. The Liberal welfare reforms began after which general election?
4. The United Kingdom fought what empire in the Gallipoli Campaign?
5. While working for Robert Samuel Wright, Herbert Henry Asquith prepared a memorandum for which Prime Minister?
6. Herbert Henry Asquith first represented what constituency as a Member of Parliament?
7. Which politician did Herbert Henry Asquith defend in 1887 and 1888 after he was charged with assaulting police officers?
8. What cabinet position was Herbert Henry Asquith appointed to in 1892?
9. In what country did Herbert Henry Asquith meet the King after being appointed Prime Minister?
10. Who served as Chancellor of the Exchequer during Herbert Henry Asquith's premiership?

Herbert Henry Asquith (expert)

1. In what years did Herbert Henry Asquith serve as Prime Minister?
2. Herbert Henry Asquith's ancestor, Joseph Asquith, was imprisoned for taking part in what pro-Roundhead plot?
3. Herbert Henry Asquith attended what constituent college of Oxford University?
4. What political magazine did Herbert Henry Asquith write for between 1876 and 1884?
5. What position did Herbert Henry Asquith appoint Winston Churchill to when he became Prime Minister?
6. The Wharf and Mill House were two houses owned by Herbert Henry Asquith in what English county?
7. What woman did Herbert Henry Asquith famously write many letters to between 1910 and 1915?
8. In what year was the Government of Ireland Act 1914 repealed?
9. The Minister of Munitions was a political position created in response to what?
10. In what year did Herbert Henry Asquith resign as Prime Minister?

David Lloyd George (easy)

1. What was David Lloyd George's nationality?

A English
B Welsh
C Scottish
D Irish

2. David Lloyd George served as Prime Minister during what war?

A Second Boer War
B First World War
C Second World War
D Vietnam War

3. David Lloyd George was the last person from what political party to serve as Prime Minister?

A Socialist
B Whig
C Liberal
D Labour

4. David Lloyd George was the first Minister of what?

A Colonies
B Trade
C Industry
D Munitions

5. What was the name of David Lloyd George's first wife?

A Mandy
B Matilda
C Margaret
D Mary

6. David Lloyd George was the only Prime Minister to…

A Speak English as a second language
B Kill someone in a duel
C Win four successive general elections
D Form a coalition government

7. How was Richard Lloyd related to Lloyd George?

A Brother
B Father
C Uncle
D Cousin

8. What was David Lloyd George's occupation before he became a politician?

A Stagecoach driver
B Farmer
C Businessman
D Lawyer

9. How many years did David Lloyd George represent Carnarvon as a Member of Parliament?

A 2
B 12
C 34
D 55

10. What political position did David Lloyd George hold immediately prior to becoming Prime Minister?

A Foreign Secretary
B Chancellor of the Exchequer
C Speaker of the House of Commons
D None

David Lloyd George (average)

1. What political office was David Lloyd George appointed to in 1905?
2. In what year did the People's Budget become law?
3. Some Conservatives referred to David Lloyd George and who else as the 'Terrible Twins'?
4. In what country was the Treaty of Versailles signed?
5. The Zimmermann Telegram proposed an alliance between Germany and what other country?
6. In what general election was the 'Coalition Coupon' letter sent to parliamentary candidates, endorsing them as official representatives of the coalition government?
7. The Representation of the People Act 1918 gave some women over what age the right to vote?
8. In what year did the Irish War of Independence break out?
9. Under what act was Northern Ireland created?
10. Compulsory rationing was imposed by David Lloyd George's government at the turn of what year?

David Lloyd George (expert)

1. In what years did David Lloyd George serve as Prime Minister?
2. What prominent world leader did David Lloyd George visit in 1936?
3. What peerage did David Lloyd George receive in 1945?
4. In what year did David Lloyd George make his last speech in the House of Commons?
5. What did David Lloyd George die from?
6. Where is the Lloyd George Museum located?
7. How many children did David Lloyd George have?
8. Who did David Lloyd George succeed as Secretary of State for War?
9. The Imperial War Cabinet met over how many sessions?
10. In what year was the National Insurance Act passed?

Andrew Bonar Law (average)

1. What did Andrew Bonar Law die from?
2. What political party was Andrew Bonar Law a member of?
3. What industry did Andrew Bonar Law work in after leaving school?
4. What country was Andrew Bonar Law born in?
5. Where is Andrew Bonar Law buried?
6. In what years did Andrew Bonar Law serve as Prime Minister?
7. In what year did Andrew Bonar Law first become a Member of Parliament?
8. What caused the deaths of Andrew Bonar Law's two eldest sons?
9. What political office did Andrew Bonar Law hold between 1919 and 1921?
10. Andrew Bonar Law served in a coalition government headed by what Prime Minister?

Stanley Baldwin (average)

1. How many times did Stanley Baldwin serve as Prime Minister?
2. Who did Stanley Baldwin succeed as the Member of Parliament for Bewdley?
3. In what year did the Carlton Club meeting take place?
4. Who served as Foreign Secretary between 1924 and 1929?
5. How many days did the 1926 United Kingdom general strike last?
6. How many monarchs did Stanley Baldwin serve under as Prime Minister?
7. The Hoare–Laval Pact was a proposal to end what war?
8. What civil war broke out in 1936?
9. Where is Stanley Baldwin buried?
10. Stanley Baldwin's father was the director of what railway company?

Ramsay MacDonald (average)

1. Ramsay MacDonald was the first Prime Minister from what political party?
2. What financial crisis took place while Ramsay MacDonald was Prime Minister?
3. Who took part in the Invergordon Mutiny?
4. In what years was Ramsay MacDonald the leader of a National Government?
5. What was Ramsay MacDonald's father's occupation?
6. Ramsay MacDonald witnessed what violent clash between police and demonstrators in 1887?
7. What was the name of Ramsay MacDonald's wife?
8. Who served as Home Secretary during Ramsay MacDonald's first term as Prime Minister?
9. What newspaper published the Zinoviev letter in 1924?
10. The British Empire Economic Conference of 1932 was held in what city?

Neville Chamberlain (average)

1. What war broke out during Neville Chamberlain's premiership?
2. What political party was Neville Chamberlain a member of?
3. What city was Neville Chamberlain born in?
4. What was the name of Neville Chamberlain's father?
5. The Munich Agreement was known by what other name?
6. Neville Chamberlain was named Minister of what in 1923?
7. Who was serving as First Lord of the Admiralty when Neville Chamberlain resigned as Prime Minister?
8. How old was Neville Chamberlain when he first became a Member of Parliament?
9. What did Neville Chamberlain die from?
10. What political position did Neville Chamberlain hold immediately prior to becoming Prime Minister?

Winston Churchill (easy)

1. How many times did Winston Churchill serve as Prime Minister?

A 1
B 2
C 3
D 4

2. Who served as Winston Churchill's Deputy Prime Minister during the Second World War?

A Neville Chamberlain
B Clement Attlee
C Edward Heath
D Anthony Eden

3. What political office did Winston Churchill hold before becoming Prime Minister?

A First Lord of the Admiralty
B Foreign Secretary
C Chancellor of the Exchequer
D None

4. Where was Winston Churchill born?

A The White House
B Blenheim Palace
C Buckingham Palace
D Edinburgh Castle

5. What was the name of Winston Churchill's wife?

A Olga
B Diana
C Clementine
D Anne-Marie

6. What was the nationality of Winston Churchill's mother, Jennie Churchill?

A French
B English
C American
D Australian

7. Winston Churchill's response to what famine generated controversy?

A Hungarian famine
B German famine
C Bengal famine
D Honduran famine

8. The bombing of Dresden in February 1945 resulted in what?

A German surrender
B A firestorm
C Hitler's suicide
D American entry into the Second World War

9. The Mau Mau Uprising occurred in what country?

A Sudan
B Kenya
C Madagascar
D South Africa

10. The United Kingdom backed a coup in what country in 1953?

A Libya
B Syria
C Iran
D Iraq

Winston Churchill (average)

1. Winston Churchill was associated with what two political parties?
2. Winston Churchill served as Prime Minister under what two monarchs?
3. What term did Winston Churchill use to describe the boundary between the Western and Soviet spheres of influence?
4. Who was Winston Churchill's nanny?
5. What boarding school did Winston Churchill attend as a child?
6. In what year was Winston Churchill commissioned in the British Army?
7. What was the name of Winston Churchill's first published work of non-fiction?
8. Winston Churchill was held as a prisoner of war during what conflict?
9. What group took part in the Tonypandy riots of 1910-11?
10. Winston Churchill was named Chancellor of the Exchequer under what Prime Minister?

Winston Churchill (expert)

1. Where is Winston Churchill buried?
2. Winston Churchill was a direct descendant of members of what dukedom?
3. Where did Winston Churchill's parents marry?
4. In what year did Winston Churchill first become a Member of Parliament?
5. Who did Winston Churchill publish a biography of in 1906?
6. What was the first cabinet position that Winston Churchill held?
7. What infantry regiment did Winston Churchill serve in during the First World War?
8. What name is often attributed to the low-point Winston Churchill's career suffered following the 1929 general election?
9. Who turned down the offer to become Prime Minister, leading to Winston Churchill being appointed to the position instead?
10. What name is commonly given to the speech Winston Churchill delivered to the House of Commons on 4 June 1940?

Clement Attlee (easy)

1. What political party was Clement Attlee a member of?

A Conservative
B Social Democratic Party
C Liberal
D Labour

2. What political position did Clement Attlee hold prior to becoming Prime Minister?

A Deputy Prime Minister
B Chancellor of the Exchequer
C Foreign Secretary
D Speaker of the House of Commons

3. What English county was Clement Attlee born in?

A Merseyside
B Lancashire
C Staffordshire
D Surrey

4. What was the name of Clement Attlee's wife?

A Mary
B Violet
C Georgina
D Jan

5. In what year did Clement Attlee win an unexpected landslide election victory, leading to him becoming Prime Minister?

A 1940
B 1945
C 1951
D 1967

6. In what year was the National Health Service founded?

A 1932
B 1942
C 1948
D 1951

7. What position did Ernest Bevin hold during Clement Attlee's premiership?

A Health Secretary
B Chancellor of the Exchequer
C Foreign Secretary
D Speaker of the House of Commons

8. British India was partitioned into what two countries in 1947?

A India and Thailand
B India and China
C India and Afghanistan
D India and Pakistan

9. Clement Attlee supported what American plan to rebuild Europe after the Second World War?

A Counter-Communist Plan
B Marshall Plan
C Monroe Doctrine
D Truman Aid

10. The Malayan Emergency lasted just over how many years?

A 2
B 5
C 12
D 34

Clement Attlee (average)

1. Who succeeded Clement Attlee as Prime Minister?
2. What position was Clement Attlee appointed to in 1935, following the resignation of George Lansbury?
3. Who served as Minister for Health between 1945 and 1951?
4. In what year was NATO formed?
5. In what year did Clement Attlee call a snap general election, leading to his downfall?
6. What war did Clement Attlee fight in?
7. Clement Attlee was trained in what profession?
8. Clement Attlee opposed what 1938 agreement between the United Kingdom and Germany?
9. Clement Attlee was the first person to hold what political position?
10. In what year was the act that nationalised railways in the United Kingdom passed?

Clement Attlee (expert)

1. Clement Attlee was first elected as a Member of Parliament for what constituency?
2. Clement Attlee was wounded during what military campaign?
3. What was the name of the first book Clement Attlee had published in 1920?
4. What political position was Clement Attlee appointed to in 1930?
5. What influential report was published in November 1942?
6. How many people served as Chancellor of the Exchequer under Clement Attlee?
7. What position did Ellen Wilkinson hold on Clement Attlee's cabinet?
8. What loan did the USA pay to the United Kingdom in 1946?
9. In what year did Clement Attlee become a member of the House of Lords?
10. In 1962 Clement Attlee spoke out against the United Kingdom's application to join what organisation?

Anthony Eden (average)

1. Anthony Eden was the Earl of what?
2. Anthony Eden served three times in what political position?
3. Anthony Eden served as Deputy Prime Minister under what Prime Minister?
4. In what years did Anthony Eden serve as Prime Minister?
5. Anthony Eden resigned from Neville Chamberlain's cabinet as a result of what?
6. The Suez Crisis involved an invasion of what country?
7. Anthony Eden was born at what country house?
8. Anthony Eden's younger brother, Nicholas Eden, died during what battle?
9. What reason did Anthony Eden give for resigning as Prime Minister?
10. The MI6 diver, Lionel Crabb, went missing in what dockyard?

Harold Macmillan (average)

1. What political position did Harold Macmillan hold prior to becoming Prime Minister?
2. What was Harold Macmillan's nickname?
3. In what year was national service ended?
4. The Polaris Sales Agreement (1963) concerned what kind of weapon?
5. Harold Macmillan was the last Prime Minister born in what era of British history?
6. What position did John Profumo hold on Harold Macmillan's cabinet?
7. How old was Harold Macmillan when he died?
8. What publishing company did Harold Macmillan's grandfather, Daniel Macmillan, found?
9. Harold Macmillan was seriously wounded in what battle of the First World War?
10. What cabinet position was Harold Macmillan appointed to in 1951?

Alec Douglas-Home (average)

1. In what years did Alec Douglas-Home serve as Prime Minister?
2. What sport did Alex Douglas-Home excel at?
3. Alec Douglas-Home was the last person to become Prime Minister while a member of what?
4. What treaty relating to nuclear weapons did Alec Douglas-Home sign in 1963?
5. What political position did Alec Douglas-Home hold prior to becoming Prime Minister?
6. After his premiership, Alec Douglas-Home served in the cabinet of which Prime Minister?
7. Alec Douglas-Home lost his seat in the House of Commons in what election?
8. What country was Alec Douglas-Home in when he died?
9. Who was assassinated shortly after Alec Douglas-Home became Prime Minister?
10. Two left-wing students from what university attempted to kidnap Alec Douglas-Home?

Harold Wilson (average)

1. Operation Banner refers to a military operation in what country?
2. What political party was Harold Wilson a member of?
3. On how many occasions did Harold Wilson serve as Prime Minister?
4. Harold Wilson refused to send British troops to take part in what major war?
5. How old was Harold Wilson when he was first photographed on the doorstep of 10 Downing Street?
6. Harold Wilson became a Fellow of what society in 1943?
7. In what year did Harold Wilson first become a Member of Parliament?
8. How old was Harold Wilson when he first became a cabinet minister?
9. What did Harold Wilson die from?
10. What name is often given to the ethno-nationalist conflict that broke out in Northern Ireland in the late 1960s?

Edward Heath (average)

1. What multinational organisation did the United Kingdom join in 1973?
2. In what years did Edward Heath serve as Prime Minister?
3. 15 February 1971 is better known by what name?
4. In what year was Northern Ireland's parliament suspended and direct rule imposed?
5. The Three-Day Week was imposed in order to limit the consumption of what?
6. Who succeeded Edward Heath as Leader of the Conservative Party?
7. Edward Heath remained a Member of Parliament until what year?
8. Where is Edward Heath buried?
9. How many times did Edward Heath marry?
10. Anthony Barber became Chancellor of the Exchequer after whose death?

James Callaghan (average)

1. James Callaghan famously served in all four of what?
2. In what years did the Winter of Discontent occur?
3. James Callaghan was the last Prime Minister born before what conflict?
4. In what year did James Callaghan hold a referendum concerning Scottish devolution?
5. What was the name of James Callaghan's wife?
6. What was James Callaghan's real first name?
7. James Callaghan controversially appointed his son in law, Peter Jay, to what political position?
8. How many votes did James Callaghan lose a vote of no confidence by in 1979?
9. What campaign slogan did Margaret Thatcher use against James Callaghan's government?
10. What Vesta Victoria song did James Callaghan famously sing at the Trades Union Congress?

Margaret Thatcher (easy)

1. Margaret Thatcher was the first person from what group to become Prime Minister?

A Working class
B Woman
C Journalist
D Dual citizen

2. What nickname is commonly attributed to Margaret Thatcher?

A Ambitious Lady
B Greedy Lady
C Iron Lady
D First Lady

3. Where did Margaret Thatcher die?

A Blenheim Palace
B Palace of Westminster
C Ritz Hotel
D Whitwick Manor

4. What political party was Margaret Thatcher a member of?

A Conservative
B Liberal
C UKIP
D Labour

5. What was the name of Margaret Thatcher's husband?

A Mark
B Denis
C Anthony
D Elliott

6. What university did Margaret Thatcher attend?

A University of St Andrews
B Durham University
C Oxford University
D Yale University

7. What country did the United Kingdom fight against in the Falklands War?

A Argentina
B Mexico
C India
D Iceland

8. What English county was Margaret Thatcher born in?

A Lincolnshire
B Leicestershire
C Lancashire
D Buckinghamshire

9. What type of shops did Margaret Thatcher's father own?

A Newsagent
B Post office
C Grocery
D Book

10. Margaret Thatcher first became a cabinet minister under what Prime Minister?

A Winston Churchill
B Anthony Eden
C Harold Wilson
D Edward Heath

Margaret Thatcher (average)

1. A leadership election was called by the Conservative Party in 1990 after whose decision to challenge Margaret Thatcher?
2. The Community Charge was commonly known by what name?
3. What terrorist group was responsible for the Brighton hotel bombing?
4. What country's London embassy was stormed in 1980?
5. What was the first cabinet position Margaret Thatcher held?
6. In what year did Margaret Thatcher become Leader of the Opposition?
7. 'The lady's not for turning' was a phrase used by Margaret Thatcher at what 1980 conference?
8. What group held a major strike in 1984-85?
9. Margaret Thatcher resisted the attempt to privatise what company?
10. What occurred at HM Prison Maze in 1981?

Margaret Thatcher (expert)

1. In what years did Margaret Thatcher serve as Prime Minister?
2. What did Margaret Thatcher die from?
3. In what year did Margaret Thatcher first campaign to become a Member of Parliament?
4. How many children did Margaret Thatcher have?
5. Circular 10/70 was an attempt by Margaret Thatcher to reverse the effects of what?
6. The Sino-British Joint Declaration was a treaty concerning what territory?
7. Margaret Thatcher was initially opposed to the reunification of what country?
8. What is the name of the memoires Margaret Thatcher published in 1993?
9. Margaret Thatcher attended whose state funeral service in 2004?
10. What peerage did Margaret Thatcher receive in 1992?

John Major (average)

1. What political position did John Major hold prior to becoming Prime Minister?
2. Where did the Irish Republican Army (IRA) attempt to assassinate John Major in 1991?
3. What major war was the United Kingdom taking part in at the start of John Major's premiership?
4. Black Wednesday occurred after the United Kingdom withdrew pound sterling from what?
5. In what year did John Major leave the House of Commons?
6. What was the occupation of John Major's father, Tom Major-Ball?
7. What company did John Major start working for in 1963?
8. In what year did John Major first become a member of the cabinet?
9. The Maastricht Treaty was a treaty signed by member states of what organisation?
10. In what town did John Major announce the Back to Basics campaign?

Tony Blair (easy)

1. What phrase did the Labour Party use under Tony Blair to distance itself from past policies?

A Onwards!
B Innovation, Innovation, Innovation
C New Labour
D New Times, New Party

2. What city was Tony Blair born in?

A London
B Edinburgh
C Hull
D Coventry

3. What is the name of Tony Blair's wife?

A Emma
B Anne
C Cherie
D Miranda

4. Who served as Chancellor of the Exchequer under Tony Blair?

A Gordon Brown
B Alastair Campbell
C John Prescott
D Dennis Skinner

5. How old was Tony Blair when he became Prime Minister?

A 30
B 43
C 51
D 78

6. How many general elections did the Labour Party win under Tony Blair's leadership?

A 1
B 2
C 3
D 4

7. In what year was the Good Friday Agreement signed?

A 1996
B 1998
C 2000
D 2003

8. What country did the United Kingdom invade in 2003?

A Iran
B Iraq
C Afghanistan
D Libya

9. What country did Tony Blair move to in 1954?

A Australia
B Canada
C South Africa
D India

10. In what country did the Omagh bombing occur?

A Iraq
B Northern Ireland
C South Africa
D India

Tony Blair (average)

1. What political position did John Prescott hold under Tony Blair?
2. Tony Blair became Leader of the Labour Party after whose sudden death?
3. In what year was a national minimum wage created?
4. What princess died shortly after Tony Blair became Prime Minister?
5. Tony Blair converted to what religion shortly after leaving office as Prime Minister?
6. What political position was Tony Blair appointed to in 1992?
7. Tony Blair was a strong supporter of the foreign policy of what US President?
8. What relating to universities was introduced in 1998?
9. Tony Blair opposed the result of what 2016 referendum?
10. Who was named Downing Street Press Secretary when Tony Blair came to power?

Tony Blair (expert)

1. What parliamentary constituency did Tony Blair represent?
2. In what year did Tony Blair deliver his maiden speech to the House of Commons?
3. Operation Barras was a military operation in what country?
4. In what year was the Blair–Brown deal made?
5. 'Yo, Blair' was an informal greeting used by George W Bush towards Tony Blair at what summit?
6. What organisation did Tony Blair establish in 2016?
7. In what year was Hong Kong given to the People's Republic of China?
8. In 2003 Tony Blair had a cameo appearance in what cartoon?
9. Prime Ministers Questions was moved to what day during Tony Blair's premiership?
10. Tony Blair's government considered knighting what Syrian leader?

Gordon Brown (average)

1. What country is Gordon Brown from?
2. What political position did Gordon Brown hold during Tony Blair's premiership?
3. In what years did Gordon Brown serve as Prime Minister?
4. In what year of Gordon Brown's premiership did a major recession hit the United Kingdom?
5. Gordon Brown left office as Prime Minister after failing to form a coalition government with what political party?
6. Who replaced Gordon Brown as Leader of the Labour Party?
7. Gordon Brown's father was a minister in what church?
8. Gordon Brown's left eye was blinded after an accident doing what?
9. Gordon Brown was a lecturer at what university between 1976 and 1980?
10. What advertising campaign was launched by the Labour Party in 2007?

David Cameron (average)

1. In what year did David Cameron first become a Member of Parliament?
2. In what year did David Cameron's government hold a referendum on the United Kingdom's membership of the European Union?
3. Who did David Cameron succeed as Leader of the Conservative Party?
4. Who served as Deputy Prime Minister between 2010 and 2015?
5. What postal service was privatised during David Cameron's tenure as Prime Minister?
6. What caused David Cameron to resign as Prime Minister?
7. Who served as Chancellor of the Exchequer under David Cameron?
8. What was notably legalised during David Cameron's premiership?
9. What boarding school did David Cameron attend?
10. Who was David Cameron's tutor at Oxford University?

Theresa May (easy)

1. What political party is Theresa May a member of?

A Labour
B Conservative
C Liberal Democrats
D Independent

2. What faith does Theresa May follow?

A Anglican
B Catholic
C Methodist
D Presbyterian

3. How many children does Theresa May have?

A 0
B 1
C 3
D 4

4. What university did Theresa May attend?

A Oxford University
B Cambridge University
C Princeton University
D University of Notre Dame

5. Who was Leader of the Opposition when Theresa May came to power as Prime Minister?

A Ed Miliband
B Amber Rudd
C Tom Watson
D Jeremy Corbyn

6. What cabinet position did Theresa May hold during David Cameron's premiership?

A Home Secretary
B Foreign Secretary
C Defence Secretary
D International Development Secretary

7. Who did Theresa May appoint Chancellor of the Exchequer upon becoming Prime Minister?

A George Osborne
B Ruth Davidson
C Philip Hammond
D Kenneth Clarke

8. After losing her majority in a 2017 snap general election, what political party did Theresa May reach an agreement with in order to stay in power?

A UKIP
B Democratic Unionist Party
C Liberal Democrats
D Labour

9. What position did Boris Johnson hold in Theresa May's cabinet before his resignation?

A Education Secretary
B Environment Secretary
C Defence Secretary
D Foreign Secretary

10. What is the name of Theresa May's husband?

A Daniel
B Philip
C Carter
D George

Theresa May (average)

1. How many female Prime Ministers were there before Theresa May?
2. What terrorist was deported to Jordan in 2013?
3. What prominent member of the cabinet did Theresa May dismiss on 1st May 2019?
4. What did the United Kingdom trigger in order to begin the process of leaving the European Union?
5. What plan concerning Brexit was published in July 2018?
6. What two votes did Theresa May survive in December 2018 and January 2019?
7. What side did Theresa May support in the 2016 European Union membership referendum?
8. Where did Theresa May work between 1977 and 1983?
9. What did the hostile environment policy aim to tackle?
10. What phrase did the Conservative Party use leading up to the 2017 general election?

Theresa May (expert)

1. Theresa May became the Member of Parliament for what constituency in 1997?
2. In what year did the Cumbria shootings occur?
3. In August of what year did major rioting take place across England?
4. What immigration related scandal occurred in 2018?
5. Who came second place in the 2016 Conservative Party leadership election?
6. Who did Theresa May appoint as the first Secretary of State for Exiting the European Union?
7. Priti Patel resigned as Secretary of State for International Development after holding secret meetings in what country?
8. Theresa May's first ministry delayed the final approval for the construction of what power station?
9. What song did Theresa May famously dance to at the Conservative Party conference?
10. Theresa May is known for wearing what kind of shoes?

Answers

Robert Walpole (easy)

1. Oxford
2. The Robinocracy
3. 2
4. Whig
5. Norfolk
6. 18
7. Tower of London
8. 1721
9. Country gentry
10. Spain

Robert Walpole (average)

1. George I and George II
2. South Sea Company
3. War of the Polish Succession
4. Caroline of Ansbach
5. Patriot Whigs
6. 1742
7. Wife
8. Clergyman
9. 10 Downing Street
10. Artwork

Robert Walpole (expert)

1. King's College
2. Houghton Hall
3. Castle Rising
4. South Sea Bubble
5. 1745
6. Corruption
7. Bluestring

8. 1742
9. Who Killed Cock Robin?
10. Ontario

Spencer Compton (average)

1. 1742-43
2. Oxford University
3. Compton Wynyates
4. Royalist
5. 0
6. Warwickshire
7. 1698
8. Speaker of the House of Commons
9. Colen Campbell
10. Wilmington

Henry Pelham (average)

1. Brother
2. Sussex
3. Catherine Manners
4. Hertford College (Hart Hall)
5. Jacobites
6. The Foundling Hospital
7. Wimbourne House
8. The peerage/nobility
9. 4
10. Whig

Thomas Pelham-Holles (average)

1. London
2. Newcastle
3. Westminster School
4. Harriet Pelham-Holles

5. Lord Chamberlain
6. 2
7. Minorca
8. George III
9. Lord Privy Seal
10. The Seven Years' War

John Stuart (average)

1. Edinburgh
2. Tory
3. Leiden University
4. Bute
5. Society of Antiquaries of Scotland
6. Mary Wortley Montagu
7. 1763
8. *Stewartia*
9. Luton Hoo
10. Grosvenor Square

George Grenville (average)

1. Buckingham
2. 1765
3. George III
4. Father
5. Wotton House
6. William Pitt the Elder
7. Richard Temple
8. Lawyer
9. John Wilkes
10. Secretary of State for the Northern Department

Charles Watson-Wentworth (average)

1. Rockingham

2. 2
3. York Minster
4. Wentworth Woodhouse
5. Stamp Act
6. Influenza
7. His nephew, William Fitzwilliam
8. Thomas Gilbert
9. Edmund Burke
10. Jacobite Rising of 1745

William Pitt the Elder (average)

1. Commoner
2. 1766-68
3. Whig
4. Westminster Abbey
5. A diamond
6. Chatham
7. The Grand Tour
8. Military
9. 1736
10. Seven Years' War

Augustus FitzRoy (average)

1. 33
2. Euston Hall
3. Royal Navy officer
4. Grafton
5. Anne Liddell
6. Corsica
7. Cambridge University
8. Anne Parsons
9. Charles II
10. 1770

Frederick North (average)

1. American Revolutionary War
2. Step brother
3. 1754
4. Anne Speke
5. Falkland Islands
6. France and Spain
7. Fox–North coalition
8. Tory
9. Catholics
10. His sight

William Petty (average)

1. Dublin
2. 1782-83
3. Shelburne
4. Secretary of State for the Southern Department
5. 2
6. Christ Church
7. Peace of Paris 1783
8. Rochefort
9. General
10. James Wolfe

William Cavendish-Bentinck (average)

1. Oxford University
2. 24 years
3. Great-great-great-grandfather
4. St Marylebone Parish Church
5. Portland
6. Weobley
7. Charles James Fox and Frederick North

8. Treaty of Paris
9. A kidney stone
10. The Peninsular War

William Pitt the Younger (easy)

1. 24
2. 0
3. 2
4. George III
5. Independent Whig
6. Napoleonic Wars
7. Great Britain and Ireland
8. Westminster Abbey
9. Cambridge University
10. George Grenville

William Pitt the Younger (average)

1. 14
2. William Wilberforce
3. American Revolutionary War
4. William Petty
5. To become Prime Minister
6. Charles James Fox
7. East India Company
8. Ireland
9. Battle of Trafalgar
10. 0

William Pitt the Younger (expert)

1. Appleby
2. The Fox-North coalition
3. Prussia and the Dutch Republic
4. 1801

5. William Hague
6. Earl of Chatham
7. Lawyer
8. John Pitt
9. Income tax
10. Catholic emancipation

Henry Addington (average)

1. France
2. Home Secretary
3. 1801-04
4. 1789
5. Physician
6. Devizes
7. Viscount Sidmouth
8. Peterloo Massacre
9. White Lodge
10. Reading

William Grenville (average)

1. 1
2. Prime Minister
3. Home Secretary
4. Baron
5. Ministry of All the Talents
6. Slave trade
7. Oxford University
8. Buckinghamshire
9. Anne Pitt
10. Conifer

Spencer Perceval (average)

1. Assassinated

2. Wife
3. Lawyer
4. Northampton
5. 1807
6. 1812
7. Richard Ryder
8. The Netherlands
9. Sir Francis Burdett
10. 13

Robert Jenkinson (average)

1. Liverpool
2. 1819
3. Tory
4. George III and George IV
5. War of 1812
6. Congress of Vienna
7. Corn Laws
8. Charterhouse School
9. Henry Addington
10. 1790

George Canning (average)

1. Portugal
2. 1827
3. Westminster Abbey
4. Tory
5. Joan Scott
6. *The Pilgrimage to Mecca*
7. Actress
8. *Anti-Jacobin*
9. The Navy
10. Robert Stewart, Viscount Castlereagh

Frederick John Robinson (average)

1. 1923
2. Yorkshire
3. Sarah Hobart
4. Lincoln's Inn
5. Home Secretary
6. Earl of Ripon
7. William Gladstone
8. Carlow Borough
9. 1827-28
10. Corn Laws

Arthur Wellesley (easy)

1. Wellington
2. 2
3. Dublin
4. Tory
5. Battle of Waterloo
6. Field Marshal
7. France
8. St Paul's Cathedral
9. 1787
10. Horatio Nelson

Arthur Wellesley (average)

1. George IV and William IV
2. Peninsular campaign
3. Catherine Pakenham
4. Eton College
5. Fourth Anglo-Mysore War
6. Maratha Empire
7. Spain

8. Ludwig van Beethoven
9. King's College London
10. Duke

Arthur Wellesley (expert)

1. Walmer Castle
2. Dangan Castle
3. Lord Lieutenant of Ireland
4. Order of the Bath
5. 1806
6. George Finch-Hatton
7. Harriet Arbuthnot
8. William Huskisson
9. Arthur Wellesley's monument in St Paul's Cathedral
10. Commander-in-Chief

Charles Grey (average)

1. Whig
2. Northumberland
3. 1830
4. The Representation of the People Act 1832
5. Trinity College
6. 1833
7. 16
8. Eliza Courtney
9. Earl Grey tea
10. Newcastle upon Tyne

William Lamb (average)

1. William IV and Victoria
2. Whig
3. Home Secretary
4. The monarch

5. Lawyer
6. Leominster
7. George Gordon Byron (Lord Byron)
8. Viscount Melbourne
9. Brocket Hall
10. Resign as Prime Minister

Robert Peel (average)

1. Metropolitan Police
2. 2
3. Oxford University
4. Bobbies and Peelers
5. 1834
6. Tamworth Manifesto
7. 10
8. Railway Regulation Act
9. Daniel M'Naghten
10. Corn Laws

John Russell (average)

1. Whig and Liberal
2. Ireland
3. Foreign Secretary
4. Pembroke Lodge
5. University of Edinburgh
6. Napoleon Bonaparte
7. Finality Jack
8. Gunboat diplomacy
9. Foreign Secretary
10. Henry John Temple

Edward Smith-Stanley (average)

1. Derby

2. 3
3. Conservative
4. Representation of the People Act 1867
5. Knowsley Hall
6. Benjamin Disraeli
7. The Who? Who? Ministry
8. East India Company
9. Conservative Party
10. National schools

George Hamilton-Gordon (average)

1. Crimean War
2. 1852-55
3. Aberdeen
4. Orphaned
5. Foreign Secretary
6. Tuberculosis
7. Austria
8. The Duchy of Lancaster
9. Peelite
10. The Charge of the Light Brigade

Henry John Temple (easy)

1. Viscount Palmerston
2. Liberal
3. 2
4. Westminster Abbey
5. William Lamb
6. Victoria
7. Crimean War
8. Westminster
9. Foreign Secretary
10. 0

Henry John Temple (average)

1. Classiebawn Castle
2. University of Cambridge
3. Edward Smith-Stanley
4. Gunboat diplomacy
5. 70
6. Second Opium War
7. Divorce
8. Napoleon III
9. Chancellor of the Exchequer
10. American Civil War

Henry John Temple (expert)

1. It was an Irish peerage
2. Harrow School
3. 1802
4. Pumice Stone
5. Cambridge House
6. Richard Lyons
7. Birkenhead
8. 1865
9. 3
10. 1861

Benjamin Disraeli (easy)

1. Jewish
2. Conservative
3. 2
4. William Gladstone
5. 1837
6. Victoria
7. Ottoman Empire

8. One nation conservatism
9. Ottoman Empire
10. Bloomsbury

Benjamin Disraeli (average)

1. Mary Anne Lewis
2. Suez Canal Company
3. Balkan peninsula
4. 1880
5. D'Israeli
6. 3
7. Constantinople Conference
8. Empress of India
9. Beaconsfield
10. Italy

Benjamin Disraeli (expert)

1. *Endymion*
2. 1817
3. Carlton Club
4. 1839
5. St Michael and All Angels Church, Hughenden
6. Isaac D'Israeli
7. Henry Colburn
8. Hughenden Manor
9. 1853
10. Archibald Campbell Tait

William Gladstone (easy)

1. Ewart
2. Liberal
3. 4
4. Liverpool

5. Westminster Abbey
6. Scotland
7. Gladstonian liberalism
8. God's Only Mistake
9. Went on the Grand Tour
10. Slaves

William Gladstone (average)

1. Catherine Glynne
2. Oxford University
3. Tory
4. Reloading a gun
5. George Hamilton-Gordon
6. Benjamin Disraeli
7. Midlothian campaign
8. Maynooth Grant
9. Church of England
10. Confederate States of America

William Gladstone (expert)

1. Classics and Mathematics
2. 1832
3. Glenalmond College
4. British Army
5. Tree felling
6. London Underground
7. Hawarden
8. The Royal Society
9. 1868
10. First Boer War

Robert Gascoyne-Cecil (average)

1. Salisbury

2. 3
3. Conservative
4. Hatfield House
5. India
6. 1889
7. Naval Defence Act 1889
8. Portugal
9. Africa
10. Transvaal Republic

Archibald Primrose (average)

1. 1894-95
2. Rosebery
3. USA
4. Liberal Imperialist
5. Hannah de Rothschild
6. Francis Douglas, Viscount Drumlanrig
7. Cordite vote
8. William Harcourt
9. Ladas
10. Mentmore Towers

Arthur Balfour (average)

1. David Lloyd George
2. Jewish
3. Conservative
4. His uncle, Robert Gascoyne-Cecil
5. France
6. Second Boer War
7. 0
8. 1874
9. The Fourth Party
10. 1906

Henry Campbell-Bannerman (average)

1. Ill health
2. Herbert Henry Asquith
3. Scotland
4. 10 Downing Street
5. National Liberal Club
6. The Education (Provision of Meals) Act 1906
7. Force Henry Campbell-Bannerman to give up his position as the Leader of the Liberal Party
8. Charlotte Bruce
9. Third class
10. Edward VII

Herbert Henry Asquith (easy)

1. Liberal
2. First World War
3. Lawyer
4. 1905
5. 4
6. Social welfare
7. The House of Commons and the House of Lords
8. 2
9. Ireland
10. 1915

Herbert Henry Asquith (average)

1. Edward VII and George V
2. West Riding of Yorkshire
3. 1906
4. Ottoman Empire
5. William Gladstone
6. East Fife

7. Cunninghame Graham
8. Home Secretary
9. France
10. David Lloyd George

Herbert Henry Asquith (expert)

1. 1908-16
2. Farnley Wood Plot of 1664
3. Balliol Collge
4. *The Spectator*
5. President of the Board of Trade
6. Oxfordshire
7. Venetia Stanley
8. 1920
9. The Shell Crisis of 1915
10. 1916

David Lloyd George (easy)

1. Welsh
2. First World War
3. Liberal
4. Munitions
5. Margaret
6. Spoken English as a second language
7. Uncle
8. Lawyer
9. 55
10. Chancellor of the Exchequer

David Lloyd George (average)

1. President of the Board of Trade
2. 1910
3. Winston Churchill

4. France
5. Mexico
6. 1918
7. 30
8. 1919
9. Government of Ireland Act 1920
10. 1918

David Lloyd George (expert)

1. 1916-22
2. Adolf Hitler
3. Earl Lloyd-George of Dwyfor
4. 1942
5. Cancer
6. Llanystumdwy
7. 5
8. Herbert Kitchener
9. 3
10. 1911

Andrew Bonar Law (average)

1. Throat cancer
2. Conservative
3. Iron industry
4. Canada
5. Westminster Abbey
6. 1922-23
7. 1900
8. First World War
9. Lord Privy Seal
10. David Lloyd George

Stanley Baldwin (average)

1. 3
2. His father, Alfred Baldwin
3. 1922
4. Austen Chamberlain
5. 9
6. 3
7. Second Italo-Ethiopian War
8. Spanish Civil War
9. Worcester Cathedral
10. Great Western Railway

Ramsay MacDonald (average)

1. Labour
2. The Great Depression
3. Royal Navy sailors
4. 1931-35
5. Farmer
6. Bloody Sunday
7. Margaret Gladstone
8. Arthur Henderson
9. *Daily Mail*
10. Ottawa, Canada

Neville Chamberlain (average)

1. Second World War
2. Conservative
3. Birmingham
4. Joseph Chamberlain
5. The Munich Betrayal
6. Health
7. Winston Churchill

8. 49
9. Bowel cancer
10. Chancellor of the Exchequer

Winston Churchill (easy)

1. 2
2. Clement Attlee
3. First Lord of the Admiralty
4. Blenheim Palace
5. Clementine
6. American
7. Bengal famine
8. A firestorm
9. Kenya
10. Iran

Winston Churchill (average)

1. Conservative and Liberal
2. George VI and Elizabeth II
3. Iron Curtain
4. Elizabeth Everest
5. Harrow School
6. 1895
7. *The Story of the Malakand Field Force*
8. Second Boer War
9. Miners
10. Stanley Baldwin

Winston Churchill (expert)

1. St Martin's Church, Bladon
2. Marlborough
3. British Embassy, Paris
4. 1900

5. His father, Lord Randolph Churchill
6. President of the Board of Trade
7. Royal Scots Fusiliers
8. The wilderness years
9. Edward Wood, Earl of Halifax
10. *We shall fight on the beaches*

Clement Attlee (easy)

1. Labour
2. Deputy Prime Minister
3. Surrey
4. Violet
5. 1945
6. 1948
7. Foreign Secretary
8. India and Pakistan
9. Marshall Plan
10. 12

Clement Attlee (average)

1. Winston Churchill
2. Leader of the Labour Party
3. Aneurin Bevan
4. 1949
5. 1951
6. First World War
7. Law
8. Munich Agreement
9. Deputy Prime Minister
10. 1947

Clement Attlee (expert)

1. Limehouse

2. Mesopotamian campaign
3. *The Social Worker*
4. Chancellor of the Duchy of Lancaster
5. Beveridge Report
6. 3
7. Minister of Education
8. Anglo-American loan
9. 1955
10. European Economic Community

Anthony Eden (average)

1. Avon
2. Foreign Secretary
3. Winston Churchill
4. 1955-57
5. His policy of appeasement
6. Egypt
7. Windlestone Hall
8. Battle of Jutland (1916)
9. Ill health
10. Portsmouth

Harold Macmillan (average)

1. Chancellor of the Exchequer
2. Supermac
3. 1960
4. Nuclear missile
5. Victorian
6. Secretary of State for War
7. 92
8. Macmillan Publishers
9. Battle of the Somme
10. Minister of Housing and Local Government

Alec Douglas-Home (average)

1. 1963-64
2. Cricket
3. House of Lords
4. Partial Nuclear Test Ban Treaty
5. Foreign Secretary
6. Edward Heath
7. 1945
8. Scotland
9. President John F Kennedy
10. University of Aberdeen

Harold Wilson (average)

1. Northern Ireland
2. Labour
3. 2
4. Vietnam War
5. 8
6. Royal Statistical Society
7. 1945
8. 31
9. Colon cancer
10. The Troubles

Edward Heath (average)

1. The European Communities (present day European Union)
2. 1970-74
3. Decimal Day
4. 1972
5. Electricity
6. Margaret Thatcher
7. 2001

8. Salisbury Cathedral
9. 0
10. Iain Macleod

James Callaghan (average)

1. The Great Offices of State (Prime Minister, Chancellor of the Exchequer, Home Secretary and Foreign Secretary)
2. 1978-79
3. First World War
4. 1979
5. Audrey Moulton
6. Leonard
7. Ambassador to the USA
8. 1
9. Labour Isn't Working
10. *Waiting at the Church*

Margaret Thatcher (easy)

1. Woman
2. Iron Lady
3. Ritz Hotel
4. Conservative
5. Denis
6. Oxford University
7. Argentina
8. Lincolnshire
9. Grocery
10. Edward Heath

Margaret Thatcher (average)

1. Michael Heseltine
2. Poll tax
3. Irish Republican Army (IRA)

4. Iran
5. Secretary of State for Education
6. 1975
7. Conservative Party Conference
8. Miners
9. British Railways
10. Hunger strike

Margaret Thatcher (expert)

1. 1979-90
2. Stroke
3. 1950
4. 2
5. Circular 10/65
6. Hong Kong
7. Germany
8. *The Downing Street Years*
9. Ronald Reagan
10. Baroness

John Major (average)

1. Chancellor of the Exchequer
2. 10 Downing Street
3. Gulf War
4. European Exchange Rate Mechanism
5. 2001
6. Music hall performer
7. London Electricity Board
8. 1987
9. European Union
10. Blackpool

Tony Blair (easy)

1. New Labour
2. Edinburgh
3. Cherie
4. Gordon Brown
5. 43
6. 3
7. 1998
8. Iraq
9. Australia
10. Northern Ireland

Tony Blair (average)

1. Deputy Prime Minister
2. John Smith
3. 1998
4. Diana, Princess of Wales
5. Catholicism
6. Shadow Home Secretary
7. George W Bush
8. Tuition fees
9. European Union membership
10. Alastair Campbell

Tony Blair (expert)

1. Sedgefield
2. 1983
3. Sierra Leone
4. 1994
5. G8 (St Petersburg, 2006)
6. Tony Blair Institute for Global Change
7. 1997

8. *The Simpsons*
9. Wednesday
10. Bashar al-Assad

Gordon Brown (average)

1. Scotland
2. Chancellor of the Exchequer
3. 2007-10
4. 2008
5. Liberal Democrats
6. Ed Miliband
7. Church of Scotland
8. Playing rugby union
9. Glasgow Caledonian University
10. Not Flash, Just Gordon

David Cameron (average)

1. 2001
2. 2016
3. Michael Howard
4. Nick Clegg
5. Royal Mail
6. European Union membership referendum result
7. George Osborne
8. Same sex marriage
9. Eton College
10. Vernon Bogdanor

Theresa May (easy)

1. Conservative
2. Anglican
3. 0
4. Oxford University

5. Jeremy Corbyn
6. Home Secretary
7. Philip Hammond
8. Democratic Unionist Party
9. Foreign Secretary
10. Philip

Theresa May (average)

1. 2
2. Abu Qatada
3. Defence Secretary, Gavin Williamson
4. Article 50
5. Chequers plan
6. Vote of no confidence
7. Remain
8. Bank of England
9. Illegal immigration
10. 'Strong and stable leadership'

Theresa May (expert)

1. Maidenhead
2. 2010
3. 2011
4. Windrush scandal
5. Andrea Leadsom
6. David Davis
7. Israel
8. Hinkley Point C nuclear power station
9. *Dancing Queen*, Abba
10. Leopard print

Also by B.R. Egginton

Non-fiction

Edward VI: England's Boy King

Edward VI's Chronicle (Edward VI)

Richard II: The Tyranny of the White Hart

The Princes in the Tower: An Enigma... 500 Years in the Making

Nicholas II: The Fall of the Romanovs

Henry Hotze: The Master of Confederate Diplomacy

Historiography for Beginners

Archaeology for Beginners

Twelve Olympians: The Greek Pantheon Made Easy

History Essay Writing Basics: For High School and Undergraduate Students

Shorthand SOS: Learn Teeline Shorthand FAST

Public Affairs for Journalists: Concise Edition

Ice Hockey Rulebook

Fiction

The Sixth Number

A Kingdom of Our Own

The Chronicles of Ascension

History Quest: The Plot

The Prince and the Pauper: Annotated Edition (Mark Twain)

Trivia

The Ultimate History Quiz

The Ultimate Mythology Quiz

The Ultimate US Presidents Quiz

The Ultimate British Royal Navy Quiz

The Ultimate English Monarchs Quiz

The Ultimate French Monarchs Quiz

www.ingramcontent.com/pod-product-compliance
Lightning Source LLC
Chambersburg PA
CBHW051357280526
45784CB00007B/2990